Original title:
The Cedar's Secrets

Copyright © 2025 Creative Arts Management OÜ
All rights reserved.

Author: Benjamin Caldwell
ISBN HARDBACK: 978-1-80567-258-6
ISBN PAPERBACK: 978-1-80567-557-0

Bonds of Earth and Sky

A bird on a branch told a joke,
It laughed so hard, it nearly broke.
The squirrel rolled eyes with a grin,
Said, "Let's do that dance again!"

The clouds chimed in with a soft roar,
While ants marched in, seeking more.
"What did the tree say to the breeze?"
"You tickle my leaves, now I feel at ease!"

Fading Footprints in the Dew

Morning mist hid many a tale,
Tiny feet left a funny trail.
"Who stepped in what?" said the old crow,
"I lost my snack in this slippery show!"

A rabbit hopped in, wearing a hat,
"Such fancy footwear—no time for that!"
The deer chuckled, nodding at the scene,
"Such silliness! What does it all mean?"

Emerald Enigmas in the Sunlight

A sunny patch, where shadows play,
Leaves gossip gossip without delay.
"Did you hear what sunlight said?"
"It claimed that dawn's just shy in bed!"

The flowers burst out in laughter loud,
With petals bright, all feeling proud.
"Why don't the daisies play hide and seek?"
"They can't stay quiet, they're far too cheek!"

The Wisdom of Whispering Leaves

Leaves gather round for a brisk chat,
"What wisdom we share!" said a fat sprat.
"I heard the wind, what a strange friend,
He blows funny thoughts, around every bend!"

A wise old oak chuckled in delight,
"Life's like a breeze, it's a funny flight.
So while we sit, let's spin a yarn,
We'll teach the stars to giggle and charm!"

Roots That Time Forgot

Buried deep in the ground,
Old roots dance all around.
They giggle in the dirt,
In their prickly, old shirt.

Whispers pass through the leaves,
Of the antics and mischiefs.
Laying claims to the past,
Sharing tales from the last.

Pigeons laugh at their stories,
Of past glories and glories.
Each twist and each knot,
Holds a secret, they thought.

So if you listen real close,
To the uproar, who knows?
There's a jest in the shade,
Where the laughter won't fade.

The Guardians of the Grove

Two squirrels hold regular court,
With nutty hats and grand sort.
Parading in their fine attire,
Chasing tales to inspire.

"Who says we're not dignified?"
One grins with a cheeky slide.
"We guard these woods with great flair,
In our acorn socks, beware!"

The birds swoop in for a show,
As the wise owls act like pros.
With witty jabs and good cheer,
In the grove, there's no fear.

Guardians of laughter and fun,
In dappled shade, they won.
With a wink and a quirk,
Nature's humor at work.

Mysteries of the Twisted Trunk

Curvy lines tell a tale,
Of gnarled paths that set sail.
As branches sway to a tune,
The trunk hums a silly rune.

"Did you see that squirrel try?
He slipped on leaves, oh me, oh my!"
Echoes of laughter ring clear,
In this trunk, joy's a souvenir.

Twists and turns hide a jest,
From nature's play, we are blessed.
Gnarled limbs sketch a grand scene,
With each twist, a giggle preen.

So gather 'round for a jest,
Let the trunk put you to the test.
For in every quirky bend,
Awaits a laugh, the best friend.

Echoes from the Tree Canopy

Up high where the branches sway,
Echoes of laughter play.
Leaves rustle, a gentle cheer,
Old secrets whispered near.

"Who hid the acorns today?"
Belfry birds all say.
In the canopy's embrace,
Every critter joins the race.

A raccoon with a sly grin,
Hides treasure with a spin.
All creatures share in the jest,
Outsmarted, they call it a quest.

So listen close, oh dear friend,
To the canopy that won't end.
With each giggle that flies,
Nature's joy never dies.

Nature's Timeless Archive

In the forest, whispers chat,
Leaves gossip 'bout the fat old cat.
Mushrooms giggle, dancing free,
Squirrels chuckle, tea for three.

Rabbits playing hide and seek,
In the shadows, Tweety squeaks.
Acorns plotting, grand schemes near,
Nature's jesters, full of cheer.

Gnarled Stories of the Forest Floor

Twisted roots have tales to tell,
Of high-flying dreams that fell.
Dirt and bugs throw a small bash,
While old stones sigh, 'What a clash!'

Pinecones giggle, brush off dust,
Rabbits rave; it's a must!
Spiders weave a web so grand,
They're the best ventriloquists in the land.

The Elusive Echo

Echoes bounce from tree to tree,
Woodpeckers rap, 'Can you hear me?'
A sarcastic owl joins the fun,
'Hoo-hoo?' he says; 'Let's outrun!'

Bubbles of laughter fill the air,
As critters giggle without a care.
Crisp leaves crackle underfoot,
Nature's humor—oh, how it's cute!

Guardians of the Quiet Glade

In the glade where laughter flows,
Gnomes play pranks that nobody knows.
A raccoon runs a snack shop here,
Selling giggles and root beer.

Owls in robes, with tiny hats,
Discussing matters, like where's the cat?
Foxes wearing shoes of gold,
Share secrets that never get old.

Unraveled Myths in the Green

In the woods, whispers speak,
Of a squirrel who claims to be Greek.
He argues with a willow tree,
About ancient lore and destiny.

A chipmunk's dance is quite a sight,
Declaring it's the next big night.
He'll host a ball beneath the stars,
With acorn hats and giant cars.

A rabbit wears a crown of twigs,
And boogies with the beetle gigs.
They laugh at tales of thunderous storms,
While plotting pranks in leafy forms.

Mysteries linger, laughter shared,
In the foliage, no one is scared.
They swap stories of days gone by,
As the moon shines and the crickets sigh.

Chronicles of the Forgotten Grove

In a glade where shadows loom,
A wise old owl found his broom.
He swept the leaves with such delight,
Stirring giggles in the night.

The raccoons dress in tuxedo style,
And strut around with cheeky smile.
They tell of treasures from the past,
While juggling apples, oh so fast.

A deer claims to be a rock star,
Singing tunes near a rusty car.
With a chorus from the crickets loud,
They form a totally goofy crowd.

Whispers float from tree to tree,
About the fun that's meant to be.
In this grove, where tales revive,
Laughter thrives, and spirits thrive.

The Lullaby of Leafy Giants

In the hush of the towering trees,
A frog croaks out a tune with ease.
His band of bugs join in a jest,
Hopping now, they all feel blessed.

A bear, with flair, wears a hat,
Ponders on why squirrels chit-chat.
He steals some honey, has a feast,
While critters toast to the funny beast.

The roots hold secrets, oh so quaint,
A little mouse who thinks he's a saint.
He tells tall tales of daring deeds,
With each small slip, the laughter feeds.

Underneath the starry glow,
They share stories, row by row.
The leafy giants sway and sway,
While everyone dances their cares away.

Secrets in the Rustling Breeze

The wind whispers sweet little lies,
To the ants that claim they touch the skies.
With tiny wings made from old leaves,
They'll soar above, or so one believes.

A turtle with speed that's purest essence,
Says he's late for an important presence.
But as he snoozes in the sun's rays,
The grasshoppers giggle and dance their ways.

Beneath the arch of tangled vines,
A lizard claims he reads the signs.
He props his shades and makes a toast,
To all the creatures who love the most.

In the rustle, wisdom's laced,
Each giggle and laugh not a moment wasted.
As stories weave through air so free,
Secrets flutter with hilarity.

Shadows of Growth and Change

In the forest, trees wear wigs,
Branches flaunt their leafy digs.
Squirrels gossip on the breeze,
About the ants' grand strategies.

Roots are tangled in a dance,
They jive and twist, they prance and prance.
Sunlight's laughter tickles bark,
While shadows play from dawn till dark.

Saplings whisper cheeky jokes,
As geese parade in lumbering folks.
The owls hoot in mock dismay,
'Why don't trees ever play the flute today?'

Twigs high-five as leaves take flight,
Celebrating each day and night.
Growth is silly, never neat,
Nature's humor can't be beat!

Scent of Ancient Wisdom

Old trees hold stories by the roots,
Whispering secrets in their boots.
With scents of pine and sage combined,
They crack jokes while we're confined.

The bark has lines like ancient books,
Fungi giggle in hidden nooks.
"Why did the acorn break the rules?"
"Because it wanted to grow big like fools!"

Moss plays hide and seek in green,
"Catch me if you can!" it teases mean.
Time's a jester with a playful grin,
Grinning wide as you breathe it in.

Crickets chirp a rhythmic beat,
As wise old trees shuffle their feet.
Nature's laugh, a fest so grand,
A secret treasure in the land!

Nature's Silent Chronicle

In the woods, a tale unfolds,
Of giggling leaves and branches bold.
Each ring a memory, each knot a laugh,
Nature's record, a silly path.

Beetles march in tiny boots,
Having meetings in leafy suits.
"Who stole my acorn?" one would shout,
"They're planning bingo, without a doubt!"

The wind comments, a playful breeze,
"Is it a tree or a house of peas?"
Sticks debate about heights and styles,
While mushrooms laugh in silly smiles.

And as the sunset paints the sky,
All creatures chuckle, wondering why.
Life's a riddle, a sweet charade,
In nature's book, joy never fades!

Tales Beneath the Bark

Underneath, where stories blend,
In cozy nooks, surprises send.
Bark's a cover for laughs galore,
Every scratch a legend, a lore.

Worms wiggle, teaching tricks,
"Don't fall, or try to do flips!"
Ladybugs boast of their small fame,
"I'm the star in this leafy game!"

Roots connect like best of friends,
Playing tag as the sunlight bends.
Every crack holds tales untold,
Of silly times from days of old.

As stars peek through the leafy lace,
The forest giggles in a quiet embrace.
Nature's antics, a merry spark,
All documented beneath the bark!

Whispers of the Evergreen Wood

In the forest where trees play tricks,
Squirrels chat in their nutty mix.
A rabbit wears a tiny hat,
He says, 'I'm fashionable, how about that?'

A woodpecker dances on his drum,
While the pinecones giggle with a hum.
The hedgehog tells jokes on sunny trails,
'The grass tickles my feet! Oh, it never fails!'

Beneath the branches, shadows twirl,
And the mushrooms gossip, giving a whirl.
A fox in glasses reads a book,
All the woodland creatures come take a look!

These woods are alive with laughter and cheer,
Whispering stories that only we hear.
With a wiggle and a jiggle, they all agree,
It's the funniest place you could ever be!

Veiled Treasures Beneath the Boughs

Hidden treasures beneath green leaves,
Giggles and gasps among the eaves.
A raccoon wearing a shiny crown,
Declares, 'I'm the prince of this leafy town!'

A colorful lizard with a funny name,
He claims he's a star in a woodland fame.
He struts and spins on a mossy stone,
Singing about treasures no one has known.

Dancing shadows with a ticklish breeze,
Teasing the flowers, the bees, and trees.
A badger shares stories with glee,
Of hidden gems beneath the old elm tree!

With laughter echoing through every nook,
These playful secrets keep us hooked.
In the heart of the green, let's take a chance,
Join the woodland revelers in their dance!

Echoes of the Ancient Sentinel

An ancient tree with wisdom so grand,
Whispers of pranks with a flourish of hand.
The owls joke late in the moonlight,
'Did you hear the squirrel? Oh, what a sight!'

Branches creak with a playful tease,
While the rabbits bounce with remarkable ease.
A crow tells tales in a comical voice,
It seems every creature has made a choice.

A chipmunk wearing boots made of cheese,
Proclaims proudly, 'Look at my speed with ease!'
The shadows stretch with a giggle and shimmy,
While tiny fairies play hopscotch, quite whimsy.

As the night air sparkles with cheerful notes,
Every critter wears jolly little coats.
Under the stars, their laughter ignites,
In echoes of joy, all woodland delights!

Secrets Wrapped in Needle and Bark

A secret hidden where the pine cones grow,
A wise old sage with stories to show.
He wears a beard made of twigs and lace,
Says, 'Come join the fun in this whimsical place!'

The toads are the audience, chilling in rows,
While the crickets serenade with tiny bows.
A fox juggles acorns with a flair,
And everybody giggles without a care.

From beneath the boughs, a riddle unfolds,
Of treasure maps made from marigold.
Who knew plants could be so sly?
A good laugh and surprise make the spirits fly!

So join in the fun, leave worries behind,
In this magical world, adventure you'll find.
With nudges and winks from the wise old bark,
Let's laugh together until it's dark!

The Hidden Heartbeat of Trees

In the forest where whispers play,
Trees gossip in their leafy way.
They chuckle as the squirrels dart,
Each branch a witness, each trunk a heart.

Roots entwined like old-time friends,
Sharing tales that never end.
With every rustle, secrets twirl,
Nature's laughter in a leafy whirl.

Sunlight dances on the bark,
While shadows plot and make their mark.
A worm debates with a tiny ant,
Who knew woodlands held such a slant?

So listen close and keep your ears,
For trees can tell of joys and fears.
In every knot and twist you'll see,
The fun in life's own mystery.

Echoes from the Forest Depths

In the depths where the echoes play,
Trees provide a comedic display.
Owls exchange their wisecracks loud,
While rabbits giggle, feeling proud.

A raccoon takes a stroll on the path,
Trip over roots, oh what a laugh!
The branches sway, the leaves applaud,
Nature's jesters, oh, they're so flawed!

Mistakes are made at every turn,
Yet lessons gleaned, there's much to learn.
With each thump, you hear them cheer,
As life unfolds, it's crystal clear.

So if you stray into this green maze,
Tune in to nature's funny phase.
For every sound, both low and high,
Is laughter echoing through the sky.

Nature's Soft-Spoken Sage

Beneath a bough, the wise one grins,
Spinning tales of losses and wins.
He'll nudge you gently, say, "Imagine,
Life's so silly! Mirth is cabin."

With squirrels plotting their nutty schemes,
And ladybugs hosting leafy dreams.
Nature delights in every jest,
Soft-spoken sage knows life's best!

The sun peeks through, and shadows dance,
Each petal prompts a merry prance.
The grass whispers jokes, unclear at best,
Yet all who hear have surely guessed.

So take a moment, find your bliss,
Join in the fun, you won't want to miss.
Nature's humor, gentle and sage,
Is laughter's spot on this grand stage.

The Hidden Narratives of the Grove

In the grove, tales are spun with ease,
Branches point at shy bumblebees.
The flowers nod, they love to share,
Little secrets floating in the air.

A deer trips lightly, a clumsy stunt,
The bushes snicker, it's quite the hunt!
Every twig has its own punchline,
As laughter wafts and makes us intertwine.

Mushrooms whisper beneath the ferns,
Plotting mischief, oh how it churns!
The breeze giggles and sways the trees,
Celebrate life with rustling leaves.

In this grove, stories unfold,
Of bark and beings, both brave and bold.
So come on in, where the fun is rife,
And learn the comedy that is life!

Caressed by the Wind's Breath

A tree stood tall, so proud and wise,
It danced with joy under clear blue skies.
The squirrels laughed, they swung with glee,
'Look at that trunk, what a sight to see!'

The branches joked, 'We're the best of friends,
Rustling secrets that never end.
With a whoosh and a buzz, we spin around,
Tickling leaves from the sky to the ground.'

The Poetry of Growing Tall

Once a tiny seed, with a dream in its heart,
Said, 'I'll reach the clouds, it's a great place to start!'
The birds sung songs to cheer him on,
'You'll be a giant, come dusk or dawn!'

And as he stretched, the critters would cheer,
'Tell us your secrets, oh tree that's so dear!'
He chuckled back, 'Just a little sun,
And a sprinkle of rain, oh, isn't this fun?'

Secrets Held in Each Ring

Count my rings, how wise I've grown,
Each year a wild tale, stories well-known.
One summer, a picnic, with ants on parade,
The sandwiches vanished, oh what a charade!

With every layer, a giggle or two,
A family of owls, all hooting for stew.
Branches wear hats made of twigs and leaves,
In the tree's wild world, everyone believes.

Melissa of the Woods

In the forest grove, there lived Melissa,
She danced with shadows, a charming miss-a.
With her tree pals, she played hide and seek,
Beneath the branches, they'd laugh and peek.

When the sun dipped low, she'd share a tale,
Of a squirrel's adventure—how he turned pale.
With each twist of the wind, they'd sway and grin,
In the forest's embrace, they were sure to win.

Unseen Life Within the Canopy

In the boughs where squirrels dwell,
A chatterbox, they weave a spell.
Acorns drop with a comic thud,
While birds hold concerts in leafy bud.

Bugs dance in a silly parade,
With tiny hats, they are not dismayed.
Ladybugs sing tunes of delight,
As shadows play peekaboo with light.

Raccoons with masks make a mess,
Raiding picnics, oh what a stress!
A hidden world, so full of cheer,
In the green realm, laughter is near.

So look up high, and you'll spot a scene,
Where nature's jesters thrive and preen.
A giggling hub, a joyous show,
In leafy worlds where mischief will grow.

A Tapestry of Green Reflections

In emerald threads, the leaves do weave,
A fabric of jokes you wouldn't believe.
Moss giggles softly, taking a nap,
While vines tangle up in a leafy mishap.

Bamboo sticks poke with a cheeky grin,
Whispers among ferns, let the fun begin!
As shadows twist like a dancer's sway,
Even nature enjoys a playful fray.

A branch snaps with a dramatic flair,
"Oops, wasn't me!" shouts the wind in the air.
Glory in green, they secretly tease,
Nature's humor, a breeze through the trees.

With sunlight poured over this joke-filled patch,
It's a laughter fest, a humorous match.
Nature's tapestry, in shades and sounds,
Where the spirit of fun always abounds.

Songs of the Wildwood

In the wildwood, tunes float sly,
A chorus of laughter, oh my, oh my!
Frogs croak ballads with silly flair,
While crickets dance with nary a care.

Woody echoes bounce from tree to tree,
"Shh! Listen close," calls out a bee.
A symphony cracked with nature's prank,
Harmony sings from the forest's flank.

Branches sway, giving a wink,
Even the thistles have time to think.
Singing their truths in giggling strains,
Wildwood magic flows in the veins.

Chirps and chortles filter through air,
Each note a jest, each beat a dare.
Underneath the canopy's embrace,
Laughter and music fill up the space.

The Unfolding of Petals

Petals unfurl with schtick and cheer,
"Ta-da!" they shout as they reveal here.
A flower holds court with a royal pose,
While others giggle, hiding their nose.

Buds play peekaboo with bees and breeze,
Economy of humor, simplicity please!
A bloom in disguise, with a joke in hand,
Sprinkles of laughter across the land.

Tulips giggle in riotous colors,
Dodging the bees like playful mothers.
Nature's humor, in pastel hues,
Dancing in gardens, as sunshine ensues.

So when petals unfold, don't just stroll,
Listen closely, let laughter roll.
In every blossom, a jest is found,
As the joy of the garden spins 'round and 'round.

Ancient Tales of the Forest

In the woods, the old tree sways,
Telling tales of funny days.
A squirrel dances, trying to fly,
While a bird just rolls its eye.

Mossy leaves start to gossip low,
About the deer who lost its flow.
Chasing shadows, it trips and spins,
Laughing out loud, as nature grins.

A wise old owl with glasses on,
Thinks it's time for him to yawn.
With a wink, he dozes off,
While tree trunks chuckle, "Oh, what a scoff!"

In this grove, secrets are a laugh,
Every creature earns its craft.
As the moon peeks through the trees,
Nature giggles in the breeze.

Bark and Breath of Time

Bark so rough, yet tales unfold,
Of trees that once were young and bold.
A raccoon sneaks with a grin so wide,
Swiping snacks, it's a daring ride!

The wise old stump claims he was spry,
Danced with fairies, oh my, oh my!
Now he sits with a pondering pose,
Wondering where all the fun goes.

Around him grow companions bright,
Whispering jokes in the fading light.
"Knock, knock!" says one with a twisty vine,
"Who's there?" "Leaf," "Leaf who?" "Leaf me alone, I'm fine!"

As laughter rises with the night,
Branches sway, feeling just right.
In this forest, joy's the rhyme,
For every creature, it's joke time!

Wisdom Wrapped in Needles

Among the needles, wisdom sleeps,
As chipmunks plot their playful leaps.
"Did you hear that?" one whispers low,
"The owls still think they're the show!"

Twirling twigs in their silly dance,
Creating chaos, taking a chance.
With every twirl, the laughter grows,
As pine cones tumble, what a show!

"Who needs a map?" a squirrel declares,
"Let's lose our way, with no cares!"
They pile on one another with haste,
Falling over, oh, what a waste!

And when the stars begin to peek,
The laughter's melody is unique.
Nature's secrets wrapped in fun,
Who knew wisdom would weigh a ton?

Hushed Rustle of Ages

In twilight's hush, the forest sighs,
Rustling leaves gossip, oh, what a prize!
A badger stumbles with comic grace,
Trying to keep its silly face.

Whispers rise, tales of old,
Of mischief and pranks, all bold.
"Why did the tree join the dance?"
"To get to the root of romance!"

The pebbles giggle, the shadows play,
While the moon's smirk lights up their way.
Old bark creaks with a joyful cheer,
As nature's laughter fills the ear.

So if you wander these ancient paths,
Join in the fun, let go of your maths.
The hush of ages brings delight,
With every corner, a burst of light!

Silence Among the Pines

In the woods where whispers grow,
Trees gossip low, you know?
A squirrel snickers, then takes flight,
As branches dance in the moonlight.

Mice play poker, chips of bark,
The owls laugh, it's quite the lark!
They trade old tales of windy nights,
With acorns as their lofty sights.

Pine cones roll like bowling balls,
The forest echoes with their sprawls.
Each creature shares a secret cheer,
And nature hums a tune we hear.

Laughter lingers on the breeze,
Among the trunks and rustling leaves.
In this realm, the funny thrives,
For in the woods, joy truly jives!

Lives Intertwined Within the Roots

Roots run deep like tangled yarn,
With neighbors sharing tales so far.
A rabbit hops to steal a glance,
While hedgehogs plot a dance-off chance.

The fox tries baking, what a mess!
Burnt biscuits lead to forest stress.
A raccoon offers tips with glee,
While the trees chuckle, oh what a spree!

Shared snacks beneath an ancient trunk,
With laughter shared and lots of funk.
Branches sway to the beat of delight,
As creatures mingle in the warm twilight.

Tangled roots, a twist of fate,
A wise old tree says, "Don't be late!"
For life's a hoot when love's around,
In this wild dance, joy is found!

The Canopy's Quiet Confessions

A canopy of leafy chatter,
Where secrets spill and laughter splatters.
The birds recount their daily flops,
While down below, the chatter pops.

A chipmunk tries a joke or two,
About acorns and the skies so blue.
But in the nest, the crows just scoff,
"Your humor's dry, come on, take off!"

Mice giggle at the clouds above,
While crickets serenade with love.
Each rustle hints at stories shared,
In this wild haven, joy is bared.

So let the whispers twinkle bright,
Amongst the trees in the soft moonlight.
With every giggle, a secret thrives,
In this canopy, laughter survives!

Time's Watcher in the Woods

An ancient tree with eyes so wise,
Has seen it all in Earth's disguise.
"Hey squirrel, where's your nut today?"
"I traded it for a dance," he swayed!

With time like honey dribbling slow,
The forest hums a silly show.
A turtle claims the title 'fast',
But winds chirp tales of races past.

The owl rolls back his sleepy gaze,
To catch the antics of silly ways.
"Why chase the moon?" asks the wise old sage,
"Laugh at the stars; they set the stage!"

In every corner, laughter spills,
Among the roots and rolling hills.
So gather round, let echoes bloom,
For time's sweet tales dispel all gloom!

Echoes of the Untold

In the forest deep, a squirrel pranced,
A secret dance, the branches chanced.
The owls blinked in disbelief,
As he twirled around, like a leaf!

Raccoons gathered, popcorn in hand,
Laughing at nuts that fell from the stand.
"You call that a dance?" one raccoon smirked,
While the dancing squirrel just quirped and jerked!

The trees chuckled, their bark so wise,
As critters shared giggles, under blue skies.
Be careful, dear friends, when you tread near,
For the laughter of nature is something to hear!

Echoes of giggles from roots underground,
In every branch, the tales abound.
So tiptoe softly, or jump with glee,
For the forest's secrets are wild and free!

Songs Flowing in the Forests

A parrot sang off-key with zeal,
Underneath a tree, his grand appeal.
"You call that singing?" the fox did crow,
"Let's hear the tree trunks, they steal the show!"

With laughter rising, the trees joined in,
Rustling leaves, they wore a grin.
Squirrels chimed in with little tunes,
As shadows danced beneath the moons!

A party erupted, a woodland spree,
With frogs providing the harmony.
The bears tapped their feet, a rhythmic stamp,
While the fireflies lit up the camp!

Through branches high, the songs would fly,
Echoes of joy in the night sky.
So join the chorus, don't be shy,
In the forest fun, we all get high!

The Canvas of Ancient Wood

On bark so old, a paintbrush swayed,
With colors bright, the forest played.
A chipmunk dabbed, using berries ripe,
Creating masterpieces, quite the hype!

The owls squinted, trying to see,
"Is that a portrait, or just a spree?"
With every stroke, the laughter glowed,
As nature's palette brightly showed!

A badger joined with mud and clay,
Mastering sculpture in a funny way.
"Behold my masterpiece! A trotting hare!"
But the art was more like, well, quite a scare!

Yet in this chaos, joy prevails,
In every splatter, laughter entails.
So let the woods be India's muse,
For joy paints smiles, we just can't lose!

Woven Whispers of Saplings

Little saplings shared tales of old,
Of starlit nights and treasures bold.
"Did you hear? The wind has a style,
It twirls and twirls, for quite a while!"

Their leaves were giggling, twisting around,
As wisdom flowed from the roots to the ground.
"The bugs have stories, they love to boast,
But we're the sassiest, it's us they toast!"

The brook chimed in with its own sweet tune,
Bubbling secrets that made all swoon.
In whispers soft, the saplings dared,
To out-fun the forest, but no one shared!

So join the murmurs, be part of the jest,
Where every creature is simply the best.
In this woodland world, where laughter beams,
Life's just a canvas, and humor streams!

Flickers of Light Through the Foliage

Sunlight winks through leaves up high,
A squirrel giggles, as passes by.
This tree's a joker, a prankster bold,
Whispers of laughter, stories old.

Birds chirp jokes, feathers askew,
A raccoon rolls, a real hullabaloo.
The breeze plays tag with every sprite,
These leafy tales dance with delight.

Roots tickle earth, a ticklish crowd,
With each new breeze, they get quite loud.
Pinecones tumble, a clumsy mess,
Nature's jesters, we must confess.

In twilight's glow, shadows prance,
A night critter's mischievous dance.
Under the moon, laughter takes flight,
Whispers of fun in the soft, soft night.

Secrets Beneath Mossy Cover

Under wet blankets, the critters conspire,
Mice pulling pranks, never tire.
Moss on a log, green velvet bed,
Frogs croak their riddles, chuckles spread.

In damp little nooks, gnomes plot and scheme,
With mushrooms for hats, it's like a dream.
They giggle as shadows play hide and seek,
Nature's comedians speak far from weak.

Worms wiggle in soil, what a delight,
Joking with roots, oh what a sight!
The laughter of ferns, an evergreen joke,
In the earth's quiet corners, humor awoke.

Mossy whispers, secrets in the air,
With every rustle, mischief's laid bare.
Together they chuckle, all through the night,
Sharing their secrets, oh, what a sight!

Nature's Memoir Written in Soil

A tale is scribbled in earthy rows,
Ants inch along, their tiny prose.
With each little step, they giggle and play,
Sharing old stories, come what may.

Each rock a character, each stone a name,
Laughing out loud in this wonderful game.
Earthworms pen verses, twisting and twirled,
Secrets of soil, they happily unfurled.

Sunbeams write notes in golden hue,
Reminding the roots of things that are true.
In each puddle, a mirror of cheer,
Nature's Memoir draws everyone near.

Bubbles of laughter rise from the ground,
With playful echoes, joy is abound.
This land is alive with vibrant delight,
Crafting its tales, day into night.

Reflections on the Bough

Up high in the tree, a squirrel plays,
Planning his winter with nutty displays.
He thinks he's a king, perched up so proud,
While birds roll their eyes, all laughing out loud.

The winds start to gossip, swirling with glee,
Whispering secrets and tickling the leaves.
One branch winks at another, what a sight!
Branches shake with laughter, under the moonlight.

A squirrel in tights? What a comical view,
He struts and he dances, all just for the crew.
His acorn crown gleams, reflecting the sun,
Oh, nature's a stage where all join in fun!

Underneath, shadows play hide-and-seek,
A light-hearted game in this bosky mystique.
The tall tales of woodlands tumble and prance,
In laughter and folly, they all join the dance.

Nature's Tapestry of Time

In woodland rich tapestries, stories unfold,
Where leaves play the chorus, their gossip retold.
A chipmunk with flair, dresses up in a bow,
While mushrooms giggle, putting on quite the show.

The flowers are blushing, caught in a tease,
As bees hum their tunes, setting time at ease.
The sun spills its warmth, a tickling ray,
While crickets do cha-cha, in a silly ballet.

Oh, the pinecones conspire, crafting a plot,
With laughter on branches, never a thought.
The tales weave together, like strands of fine thread,
In the fabric of nature, silliness spread.

As twilight drapes softly, stories abound,
Twinkling stars peek, from their dorms underground.
The jests of the woods leave all spirits bright,
In a tapestry woven, with joy and delight.

Stories Etched in Shadows

In the dappled light, shadows prance and spin,
A raccoon with mischief, cheeky grins on his chin.
He rummages through treasures, a mystical find,
While owls cast their judgment, with wisdom unkind.

Across the moonlit glade, footprints appear,
Who left that dessert? It's so crystal clear!
Berries are missing, oh what a plot twist,
Nature's great heist, and no one can resist!

As creatures convene, under stars bright as day,
Each shares their own antics, in humorous sway.
The wise old toad croaks in a deep, raspy tone,
That laughter's the marrow, in all that we've grown.

In shadows alive, the secrets unfold,
With chuckles and giggles, both gentle and bold.
The tales that are spun by the flicker of night,
Bring forth a chorus, a joyful delight.

Harmonies of Life and Decay

Underneath the leaves, a concert begins,
In the orchestra of life, everyone wins.
A beetle on bass, strumming up quite the beat,
While fireflies dance, with analytics sweet.

The old tree chuckles, as worms do their jig,
Their earthy ballet is nothing too big.
Mushrooms all gather, talking fungi chat,
In a raucous debate, on who's fatter than fat.

As petals fall down, like confetti in play,
The cycle of life loves a humorous sway.
The wind carries tales of old friends in the sky,
With chuckles and echoes of laughter, oh my!

In the fabric of nature, every note has its space,
Even in decay, we all find our place.
So lift up your spirits, let merriment reign,
Life's quirks are the treasures we all can sustain.

The Voice of the Old Growth

In the forest where trees do chat,
Old trunks gossip about this and that.
"I saw a squirrel wearing a hat!"
"Oh please, don't start that silly spat!"

Branches wave to passersby,
"Step right up! Don't be shy."
Pinecones roll, as if to fly,
Jokes are cracked, and laughter's high.

Acorns toss their tiny jokes,
While birds mimic the nearby blokes.
"Who needs a stage for silly strokes?"
Nature's humor; oh how it pokes!

Underneath the emerald shawl,
Even the roots have tales to tell.
With every rustle, giggle, and squall,
Old growth whispers the funniest spell!

Nature's Silent Chronicles

In the stillness where whispers dwell,
Nature spins stories on her carousel.
Grasshoppers dance—oh can't you tell?
They're practicing for a musical swell!

Leaves giggle with each gentle gust,
"Oh look, there's a worm with a lust!
He tried salsa, but oh, what a bust,
Two steps forward, then ate all the dust!"

A bear does yoga; what quite a sight,
While hedgehogs huddle, plotting tonight.
"Who'll win the race? Who's got the might?
Maybe the tortoise, if he's feeling right!"

Birds create tunes both silly and sweet,
As the chorus of frogs taps their webbed feet.
Nature laughs, with no need for a seat,
In this world, the joy is quite a feat!

Sheltering Secrets Among Stalks

Under the leaves, shadows do dance,
A gopher named Gerald took a chance.
He wore sunglasses for that cool glance,
Declared, "I'm here for a stylish prance!"

The flowers giggle at the bumblebee,
Buzzing around all carelessly.
"Why don't you just take it easy, see?"
To which he replies, "I'm busy, can't you agree?"

Tall stalks nod and shift with glee,
Holding secrets for the ants to spree.
"Oh look, there's a butterfly!" says a wee,
With a grin that says, "This blooms for free!"

Roots dig deep, where jokes don't tread,
Even the compost dreams up some bread.
In this green world, laughter is fed,
As each stalk shares a giggle instead!

A Symphony of Swaying Branches

Swaying branches create a tune,
An orchestra of leaves by the light of the moon.
"Let's play hide and seek!" says a raccoon,
Under the stars, laughter bursts like a balloon.

Frogs join in, with their ribbits and croaks,
They've written a song about old joke folks.
"Who is the funniest among the blokes?"
They say the owl, but he only hoaks!

The wind carries melodies, soft and light,
While critters gather for the evening's delight.
"Do you think the tree can take flight?"
With laughter echoing into the night.

As the night deepens, the giggles grow wide,
Nature's antics, she cannot hide.
In each murmur, fun is applied,
A symphony of joy forever implied!

Nature's Keeper Beneath the Stars.

In the woods at night, a squirrel took flight,
Chasing shadows, a comical sight.
With acorn armor, he felt quite bold,
But tripped on a root, oh, tales to be told!

The owls all chuckled, with feathers so ruffled,
As he flipped in the air, his dignity shuffled.
A moonlit giggle rippled through trees,
Nature's own jester, playing with ease.

Beneath the stars shining, the laughter's a glow,
Fun in the forest, just go with the flow.
Animal antics, they're easy to see,
When nature's the keeper of giggles and glee!

So if you wander where the wild critters play,
Expect silly dances at the end of the day.
Align with the echoes of joy in the dark,
In Nature's grand keeper, there's always a spark!

Whispers of the Evergreen

In a forest so green, the pine trees conspire,
Whispering secrets, they fan a soft fire.
A raccoon in pajamas sneaks up for a snack,
But the squirrels all giggle, 'He's not coming back!'

They toss little pine cones, a game they all share,
While the raccoon looks puzzled, scratching his hair.
'What's all the fuss?' he asks in surprise,
'Oh don't mind us, bud, it's just our disguise!'

With needles that tickle and bark that can laugh,
The trees spin a tale of the forest's own staff.
Whispers of breezes serenade through the night,
While critters hold court under pale silver light.

So next time you wander near towering pines,
Listen for laughter in the sun's golden lines.
The woods are a comedy, a whimsical show,
Whispers of the evergreen, ready to flow!

Enigma Beneath the Boughs

Beneath tangled boughs, a shadow does creep,
A cat in a cape, oh, what a big leap!
He prowls like a ninja, all stealth and pride,
Yet trips on a twig, oh, where will he hide?

With leaves whispering secrets of laughs gone astray,
The forest bursts into giggles that day.
The wise old owl grins, with a twinkle so bright,
He loves to tell tales about this funny sight.

In mid-air he flails, so graceful, so grand,
As the woodland critters all gather to stand.
They cheer for the feline who chose such a quest,
Only to discover he's not the best guest!

With mysteries lurking in the shadows and light,
Nature's own enigmas take wing in the night.
So take a small peek beneath boughs so green,
And enjoy all the weirdness that nature can glean!

Shadows in the Canopy

In the canopy's shadows, a party unfolds,
Where owls wear top hats and laughter is bold.
Rabbits in bow ties attempt to do dance,
But trip over roots in a flurry of prance.

The chipmunks all cheer with their tiny applause,
As the raccoons critique with wise little jaws.
'Now watch the hips sway!' says a wise old hare,
While the others just chuckle at the sight of his flair.

There's mischief and mayhem, a ruckus of glee,
In the sun-dappled glen, where all can be free.
When shadows come alive, the laughter can zoom,
As nature spins tales in the forest's grand room.

So join in the merriment, don't be too shy,
In the shadows, sweet friends, you'll learn how to fly.
A furry cabaret, it's a joyous decree,
Where shadows in the canopy set laughter free!

The Language of Sap

In the forest's playful chat,
Saplings gossip, where they're at.
Trees with secrets, oh so sly,
Whispering tales to the sky.

A pine gave a nod, with a chuckle,
While the oaks danced, oh what a struggle.
A squirrel piped up, loud and clear,
'Who's been stealing my acorn beer?'

Laughter echoed through the leaves,
As the birch teased, 'Watch out for thieves!'
With a rustle, the maples sway,
'We all know sap's the best for play!'

And thus, in their woodsy banter true,
The trees had fun, just me and you!
In this realm of roots and bow,
Life's a jest, take a seat, and how!

Fables Carved in Timber

Once there was a tree so grand,
Its bark held tales across the land.
A wise old owl would come to speak,
'Listen close, you'll hear the sneak!'

A chipmunk claimed he found a shoe,
'On my morning stroll, oh who knew?'
The alder laughed, its branches shook,
'That's the forest's best-kept book!'

Each carve and knot a funny twist,
Of lovers lost and snakes that kissed.
The fungi giggled on the floor,
'You tree folk always ask for more!'

So if you wander where they dwell,
You'll hear their stories, laugh, and yell.
In the timber, fables lie,
A ticklish tale, just passin' by!

Secrets of the Sylvan Shade

Underneath the leafy dome,
The critters gathered, far from home.
A wise old tree with limbs so wide,
Said, 'Come, friends, it's time to bide!'

A rabbit boasted of a leap,
While raccoons laughed, not missing sleep,
'Last week,' one said with a grin,
'I stole a shoe and called it sin!'

From acorns' scritch to branches' sway,
They spun their tales throughout the day.
A squirrel claimed he saw a ghost,
And all agreed they loved him most!

So find the shade, and don't be late,
Join in the fun; it's simply fate!
In this woodland's secret nook,
You'll find humor in every nook!

Veil of Green Whispers

Behind the leaves where shadows play,
The giggles hide, come join the fray.
With whispering winds and sprightly tunes,
The trees share secrets with the moon.

A leaf said, 'Did you hear the jest?',
'The beaver tried to build a nest!
But ended up stuck in muck below,
Oh, he squealed like a tinny show!'

The moss, it chuckled, cushy and soft,
As crickets chirped from trees aloft.
Their laughter danced on gentle air,
With echoes of joy beyond compare.

So lift the veil; step in with glee,
Among the whispers of the tree.
For in this realm of green delight,
Every secret's a joke, just right!

Treading Lightly Under Boughs

Underneath the leafy dome,
Squirrels hold a lofty throne,
They chatter, gossip, plan their heist,
Stealing nuts like seasoned fliers.

Pinecones tumble, a playful scene,
One hits a toad—a quarrelsome bean,
He croaks back with a venomed jest,
"You'll need a helmet, at your best!"

Frolicking in the shadows laid,
A raccoon jigs—a dapper charade,
He tips his cap, then gives a wink,
Lessons learned? Just smile and think!

With every step, a laugh ahead,
In Nature's circus, we leap instead,
So skip and hop, don't be too shy,
For dancing trees are all nearby!

The Labyrinth of Woodland Wisdom

In the moody woods, a maze unfolds,
Where trees share tales that never grow old,
A wise old owl sports a mismatched sock,
"Fashion's a game, but I outsmart the flock!"

The path twists and turns, but don't lose your cheer,
A hedgehog shouts, "I'm the guide over here!"
He rolls all around with a spiny old grin,
"Follow my lead, we'll surely win!"

A squirrel springs forth with a nutty delight,
"Hold my acorn, I'm taking flight!"
He bounces about like he's had too much tea,
And suddenly, dear friends, we're all caught in glee.

Down the path of hilarity we go,
With each step, we let our laughter flow,
So join this wild, whimsical spree,
In the woodland's labyrinth, it's just you and me!

Guardians of the Nature's Archive

Among the trees, old guardians chat,
A smart-tailed fox dons a historian's hat,
"I know every secret, each story, each bark,
Of the midnight dance and the dawn's early spark!"

A wise old turtle, slow but astute,
Records the news like a nature suit,
He scribbles on leaves with a twig for a pen,
"The best tales are often repeated again!"

The owls roll their eyes; they can't snooze,
"We haven't a break with this mob of fun news,
Let's claim some respect, with a tale of our own,
That even the saplings will know on their throne!"

As moonlight glimmers, laughter fills the air,
Tomorrow's version? A fox would declare,
"With stories so wild, you'll forget your old time,
We'll pause all the drama—let silliness rhyme!"

The Breath of Timbered Tales

A tree breathed deeply of sun and of air,
And burst forth with stories, for all who would care,
"Listen up, critters, my tales drift like breeze,
Of acorns and antics that tickle with ease!"

The rabbits perk up, with ears all a-twitch,
"What's next in your yarn? A tail that's a glitch?"
"Well, once I had branches that waved to a crow,
He mistook my bark for a dance show!"

The evening spread laughter, and shadows grew long,
As wind brought more whispers, joining the song,
"So gather 'round, friends, to share and to joke,
In the breath of my being, new laughter awoke!"

The night draped a quilt of whimsical cheer,
And backed by the stars, tales threaded near,
So under these boughs, with giggles and glee,
Whimsy and nature make magic carefree!

The Language of Leaves and Moonlight

In the night, leaves start to chat,
Whispering tales, as cats tiptoe and spat.
Moonlight shines, a spotlight bright,
While branches dance in delight.

Squirrels gossip, share acorn finds,
Beneath the stars, with playful minds.
With every breeze, secrets unfurl,
Nature's theater, a lively swirl.

Crickets chirp with comedic flair,
While owls hoot, like they just don't care.
The wind joins in, a jubilant tune,
As leaves giggle beneath the moon.

So listen close to the rustling show,
Where the trees know things we'll never know.
With a wink and a flutter, they all conspire,
To make the night a laugh-filled choir.

Heartbeats of a Timeless Giant

In the forest stands a giant old,
His heartbeats echo, tales untold.
With roots so deep, he muffles a sigh,
As squirrels scamper and birds fly high.

He chuckles at jokes of the Newton's apple,
While brushing off branches, quite like a chapel.
With each creak and groan, he shares a jest,
'The sun's my hairdresser, I look my best!'

Rabbits hop by, caught in a trance,
Wondering if they should take a chance.
To tickle the bark, just for a laugh,
Got to love that old giant's wooden path!

In the shade, secrets bend in the breeze,
Tickling the funny bones of the bees.
A rhythm of laughter, he sways with ease,
Becoming the punchline in nature's tease.

Hidden Stories of the Woodland

In the woods, where shadows play,
Hidden tales within the fray.
Woodpeckers drum a silly beat,
While raccoons dance on tiny feet.

The river giggles, weaving its way,
Snagging the gossip from night to day.
Frogs croak puns, crooners of the pond,
Their humor flows, of which we are fond.

Moss-covered logs hold their laughter tight,
As fireflies twinkle, sparkling bright.
The trees overhear secrets so sly,
Each rustling leaf lets out a sly sigh.

So wander along where the fun never ends,
Each twig a story, each branch a friend.
In the woodland's embrace, you will find,
The whimsical tales that nature designed.

Traces of Nature's Quiet Watcher

In the twilight, shadows blend and meld,
Nature's watcher, mysterious, compelled.
With eyes that twinkle like starlit skies,
He chuckles softly, beneath moonrise.

Every footprint, a quirky jest,
Who stole the berries? We'll never guess.
Leaves might tattle, but they're sworn to hush,
While laughter bubbles beneath the brush.

The nightingale sings a ballad of glee,
As beings gather, a felt jubilee.
Peeking through branches, the watcher winks,
Then scurries away, leaving us to think.

In the silence, secrets stir and blend,
The quiet watcher, our whimsical friend.
In nature's realm, humor is the guide,
In leafy whispers, where joy abides.

Nature's Memoirs in Swaying Limbs

In a forest where the squirrels play,
The trees gossip in a breezy way.
Leaves wiggle with a cheeky flair,
Whispering tales that hang in the air.

A chipmunk once stole a wise owl's pen,
And the owl cried, 'Oh dear! Not again!'
Branches chuckled, their laughter so light,
As woodpeckers danced in the soft twilight.

Mossy carpets, a cushion for pranks,
Each root a gnome, in leafy banks.
Nature's memos tucked away tight,
In knots and twirls, out of sheer delight.

Squirrels in tuxedos, the dress code clear,
Throwing a party, it's almost the year.
Rabbits in bow ties, such stylish airs,
Nature's memoirs undercover, in pairs!

A Sanctuary of Silent Revelations

In a grove where the shadows giggle,
Frogs croak jokes that make you wiggle.
Here, whispers echo in a funny tone,
As trees hold secrets, all on their own.

Bees buzz about with a rhythm so sweet,
Like they're rehearsing for a show, oh what a feat!
Ants in tuxedos, marching in line,
Carrying lunch, plotting to dine.

A tortoise tells tales, although he is slow,
Of races with hares and a quirky flow.
The sun winks bright, it's quite the charade,
In this sanctuary, dreams are parade.

Mushrooms serve snacks at a funky retreat,
With a side of laughter and pollen for sweets.
The branches sway soft, shares laughter of kin,
In this playful place where giggles begin!

Beneath the Shade of Wisdom

Under branches that tickle the sky,
Wise old trees chuckle as clouds drift by.
A raccoon with glasses reads tales of old,
While the sun offers warmth, a sight to behold.

Lizards do yoga on stones oh so chill,
While frogs give advice on how to be still.
The breeze carries whispers, a spirited jest,
As critters hold council, their sphere of rest.

Beneath boughs of wisdom, mischief awakes,
With acorns and giggles, let's share these breaks.
A hedgehog suggests we host a grand feast,
With berries and nuts, all creatures, at least!

The laughter rolls on, like a stream in play,
Each secret revealed, in a fun-tastic way.
Nature unfiltered, a party so bright,
In the shade of wisdom, pure delight!

Enchanted Half-Lights and Shadows

In realms of dusk where the shadows prance,
Fireflies twinkle, inviting a dance.
A gnome in the corner tries to keep up,
While crickets compose with a teacup.

Moonbeams giggle while weaving through trees,
As branches sway softly, teasing the leaves.
Tiny owls, with their big, bulging eyes,
Are giggling at secrets, oh what a surprise!

Nutty debates between mushrooms so round,
As shadows throw parties, where nothing's profound.
In enchanted half-lights, laughter does bloom,
As whispers of fun scatter across the gloom.

So here in the twilight, where joy can abound,
Nature's comedy show keeps spinning around.
Underneath stars, with giggles in tow,
The night brings a tale only creatures can know!

In the Embrace of Nature's Keeper

In a forest so broad, where squirrels play,
A tree wore a hat, come join the fray!
Its branches waved slowly, trying to dance,
Barking out laughter, it took a chance.

A bird chirped jokes, oh how they sang,
The roots all chuckled, and twigs just sprang.
The sun peeked in, with a wink and a blink,
Joining the fun, it began to think.

The leaves wore socks, oh what a sight!
A party of colors, both funny and bright.
Nutty acorns dropped, like confetti in glee,
Nature's own comedy, just wait and see!

So gather your friends, and take a seat,
With trees as comedians, you can't miss a beat!
In the embrace of the pines, where laughter grew,
Nature's own jesters, bringing joy anew.

The Enigma of the Tallest Trees

Here stand the giants, so high in the air,
With crowns made of leaves, like they just don't care.
They mumble all day in a husky old tone,
Plotting the weather, or guessing on loan.

One claimed a cloud, to be its new friend,
While another swayed slowly, hoping to blend.
'I'm taller than you!' one said with a grin,
Measuring hugs, determined to win.

The bark had a tale that no one could hear,
Of squirrels in tuxedos, a very fine year.
With roots on a quest, beneath all that fuss,
They found comic gold—nature's own plus!

So if you should wander, just pause for a chat,
With those towering wonders, who wear quite the hat.
Funny quirks hidden in foliage vast,
The tallest of trees hold laughter so fast.

Roots That Know the History

Deep in the ground, where shadows meet light,
The roots spin stories, both silly and bright.
They whisper of critters, and antics afoot,
Of rabbits in dance shoes, all dressed in soot.

Beneath every trunk, there's laughter and cheer,
'Did you hear the one about the deer with a beard?'
They chuckle and wiggle, with tales oh so funny,
While the soil just giggles, like it's all made of honey.

The past lives below, with secrets untold,
Of frolicsome ferns and brave marigold.
Each twist and each turn, a tale to bestow,
Funny roots sharing their wisdom on show.

If you dig a bit deeper, you might just find,
The punchlines of nature, ever so kind.
So listen intently, with all of your might,
To the roots reminiscing, from morning till night.

Whispers from the Timbered Giants

In the midst of the woods, where silence breaks free,
The timbered giants gossip, as loud as can be.
Their trunks twist in laughter, a ticklish delight,
While the wind joins in, just taking flight.

'What's with that owl, always hooting away?
Doesn't he know it's best to just sway?'
The branches all chuckled, a rustling sound,
As creatures listened closely, all gathering 'round.

They buttered the breeze with wisecracks galore,
Filling the forest, a humor encore.
Nature's own jesters, in a leafy attire,
Tickled the underbrush, as never before.

So next time you're walking, take time to discern,
The whispers of giants—a twist and a turn.
In the heart of the woods, where the jokes never cease,
Laughter grows freely, a delightful release.

The Canvas of Nature's Paint

In the forest's grand display,
A squirrel dons a beret,
Painting acorns like a pro,
Making art with quite the show.

Frogs are frequent critics, too,
Ribbiting 'What's that hue?'
Trees giggle in their leafy caps,
As branches join the happy claps.

The sun shines bright, a golden brush,
While butterflies create a hush,
They flutter by, with grace to flaunt,
Adding flair to nature's jaunt.

So grab a twig and join the fun,
Let's paint our world 'til day is done,
In this wild gallery of delight,
Where every creature's a highlight.

Layers of Life in the Forest

Beneath the leaves, a tale unfolds,
With mushrooms dancing, cousins bold,
A spider spins its tiny dream,
Crafting webs that catch the gleam.

The critters tease the trees above,
'How's it feel to be so loved?'
The roots respond with a wink,
'We're the anchors, don't you think?'

Frogs debate on lily pads,
About the latest tree-climbing fads,
While deer hold casting calls at dusk,
'We're elegant! And never brusque!'

In layers stacked, their stories blend,
Nature's humor has no end,
For every plight, there's laughter shared,
In this forest wild and cared.

Resilient Stories of the Earth

An old rock grumbles, 'I've seen it all,'
From dinosaurs to nature's brawl,
With tales of thunder and storms that roared,
He offers wisdom we all adored.

A busy ant, with plans so grand,
Speaks of fortresses he's built by hand,
'Join my parade, it's quite the sight,
With tiny feet, we'll march all night!'

Gophers chuckle, taking digs,
While owls watch with frantic jigs,
'Who's got the best story to tell?
A wise old tree or a pickle spell?'

In nature's realm, the laughs resound,
Life's resilient, and joy is found,
From rocks to ants, they all agree,
A good joke always sets you free!

The Significance of Slow Growth

A tiny seed sat snug and tight,
Dreaming of a future bright,
While ants strolled by with tales of haste,
They chuckled, 'You've got time to waste!'

A snail ambled slowly along,
Singing a sweet and mellow song,
'Why rush when life's a gentle race?
I take my time, there's joy in space!'

The trees above whispered down low,
'We've taken years to put on a show,
Let them rush, they won't know the thrill,
Of budding blooms that time fulfills.'

So slow and steady wins the game,
In nature's world, it's never lame,
With laughter echoing, soft and sweet,
Fun unfolds with every heartbeat.

Shadows of Silent Guardians

In the forest deep and wide,
Whispers dance, the trees confide.
Squirrels gossip, birds delight,
In a game of hide and fright.

Branches creak, the laughter grows,
Beneath their bark, a secret shows.
How do they know just where to swing?
Must be the best-kept gossiping thing!

Mossy carpets, fairy pranks,
Raccoons plotting, giving thanks.
For every nut and berry boast,
They hold a very leafy toast.

So tiptoe soft, don't be too loud,
These guardians stand, tall and proud.
And if you hear them chuckle near,
It's just the trees—don't disappear!

Treetop Tales in the Wind

Up above, where whispers fly,
The branches wave, the squirrels sigh.
They spin their yarns of nuts so grand,
In a world that's ever unplanned.

Leaves in chatter, flutter, and swoosh,
What's the secret? There's no rush!
A secret club, close-knit and tight,
Discussing acorns well into the night.

With every gust, a giggle shared,
Beneath the sky, unprepared.
The owls hoot, they find it odd,
While wise old trees just give a nod.

But if you dare, climb up so high,
Join the fun, let laughter fly.
For in this canopy, all's a game,
And nature's humor has no shame!

Mysteries of the Forest Keeper

Amongst the shadows, secrets lie,
A clever fox with a glint in his eye.
He knows the tales the trees will tell,
Of hidden places, enchanted well.

The roots are giggly, the vines, playful,
Nature's riddle, never stale.
The beetles joke, the butterflies tease,
As they flutter through the dancing leaves.

Whispers echo—who's the sage?
A turtle spinning stories from age to age.
With every blink, there's more to see,
A zany world, just like a spree.

So don't be shy, embrace the jest,
In nature's heart, it's a lively fest.
With laughter ringing, wild and free,
The keeper's presence is fun to see!

Beneath the Canopy of Time

Underneath the leafy dome,
The creatures prance, they feel at home.
Time drips slowly, a gooey treat,
Where squirrels slide on barky seats.

Acorns tumble, giggles echo,
Mirthful games with a forest flow.
Watch out for the frog's big show,
He hops and croaks, a forest pro!

The vines all sway like dancers fine,
And twigs crack jokes like aged wine.
In every rustle, laughter wakes,
A colorful world, from roots to flakes!

So lift your heart, and join the rhyme,
In nature's mirth, we dance through time.
With every breeze, a playful tease,
The spirits here are sure to please!

www.ingramcontent.com/pod-product-compliance
Lightning Source LLC
Chambersburg PA
CBHW051633160426
43209CB00004B/625